GREG ANDERSON

Carmen Fantasy

Fantasy for two pianos based on themes by GEORGES BIZET

for Carl Berdahl

Published by Awkward Fermata Press.
www.gregandersonpiano.com

Published 2024.
First edition published 2010. Second edition 2024.
Printed in the United States of America

Public performance licensed by ASCAP.

ISBN-13: 978-0-9830625-1-6

Carmen Fantasy for Two Pianos

based on themes by Georges Bizet

for Carl Berdahl

GREG ANDERSON

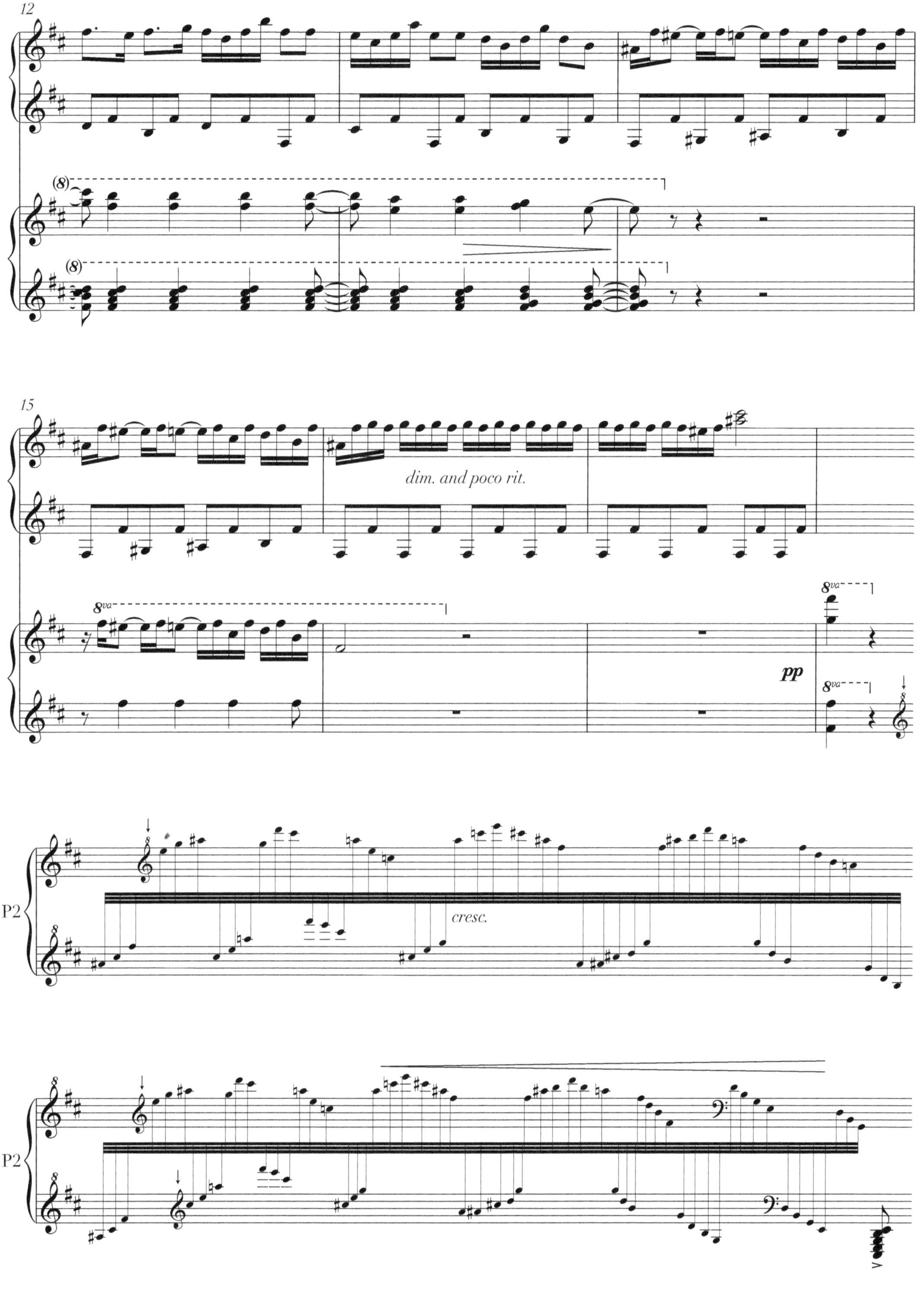
12
(8)
(8)
15
8va
dim. and poco rit.
pp
8va
8va
P2
cresc.
P2

Allegro Vivo. With a swagger ♩. = 72

5

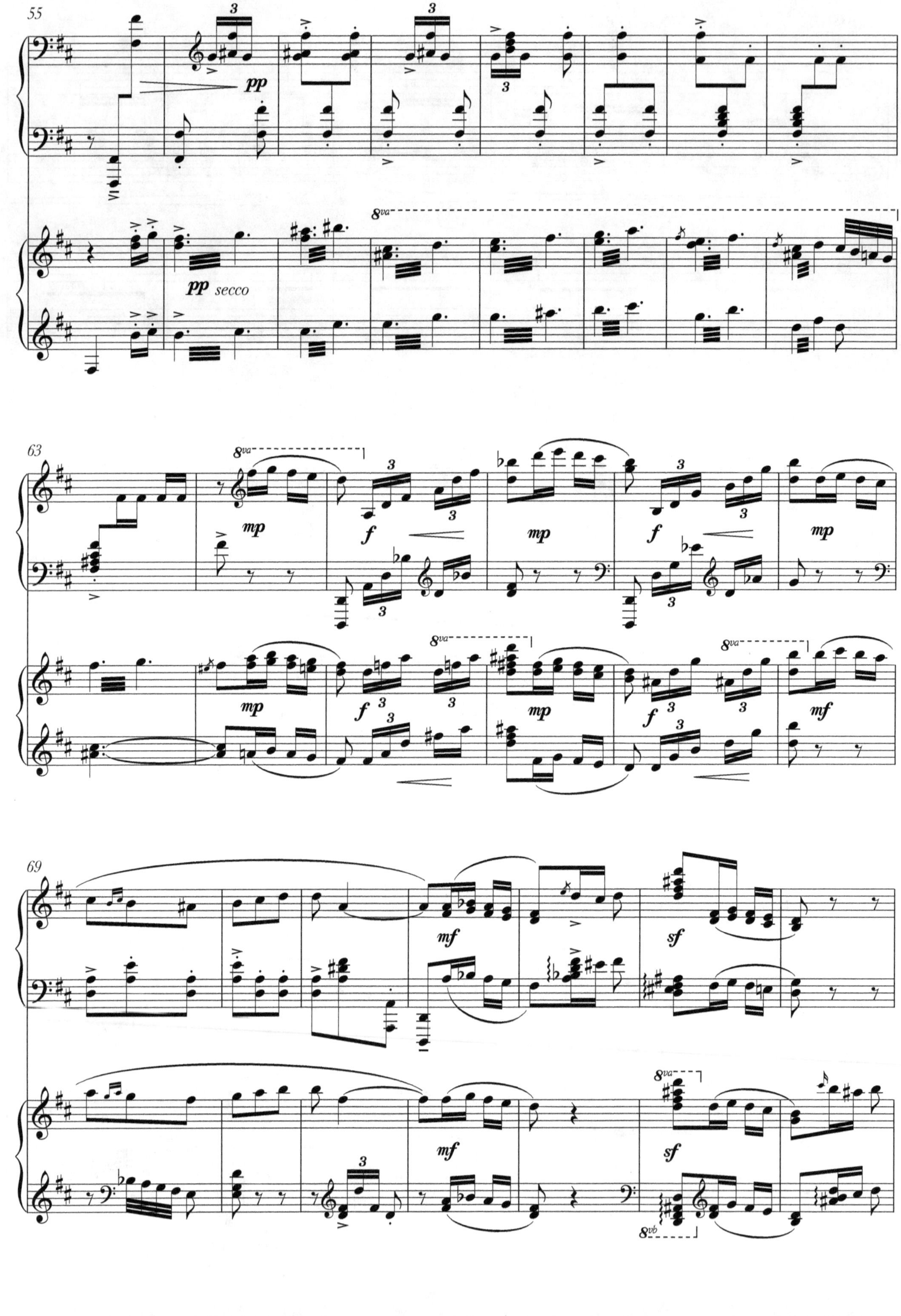
55
pp
8va
pp secco
63
mp
f
mf
69
sf
8vb

76
pp
sf p
3
with authority
sf
5
gliss.
white keys
83
f
Ped.
ff
8va
88
p
mp

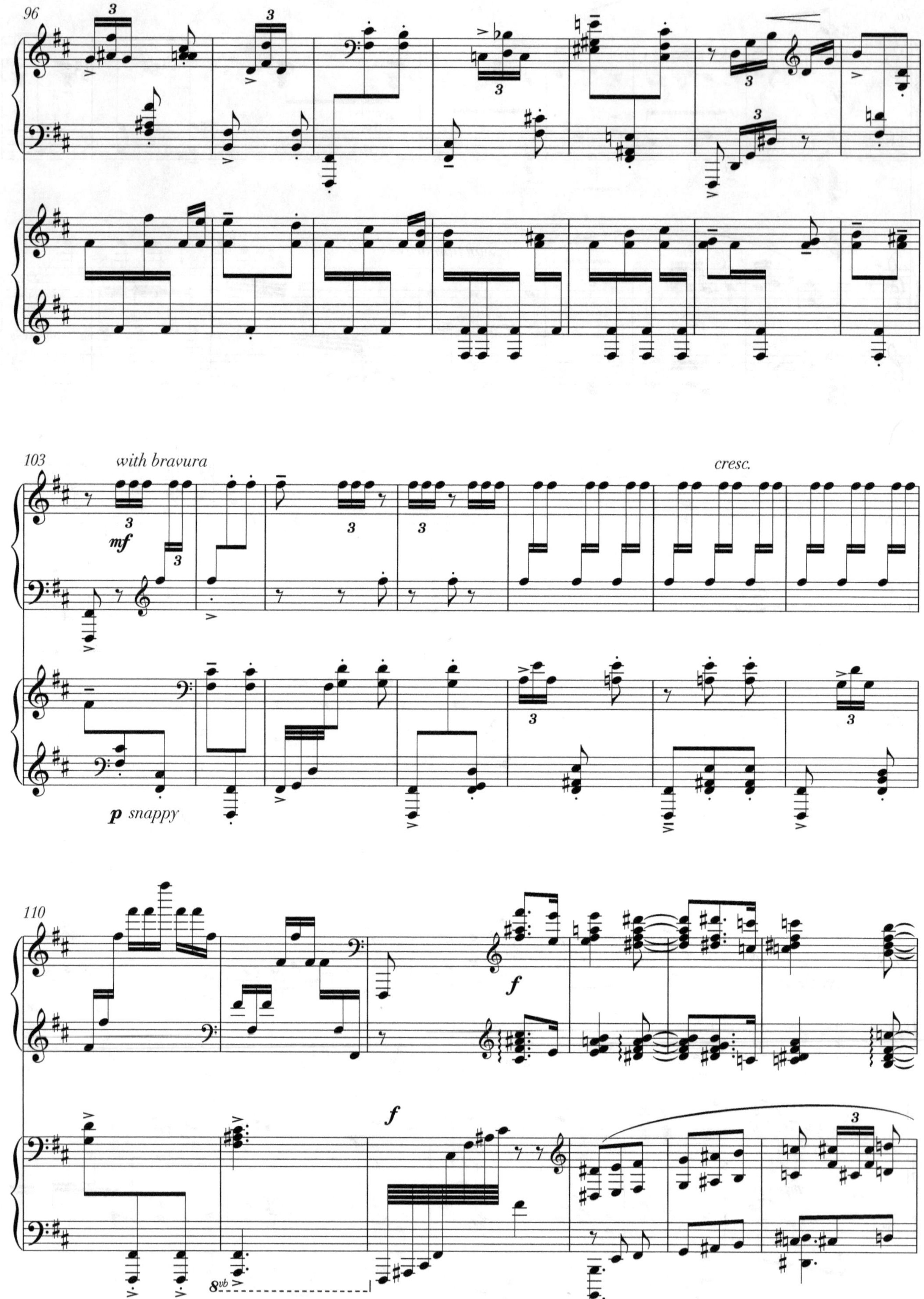
96
103
with bravura
mf
cresc.
p snappy
110
f
f
8vb

116
allagrando
a tempo
8va
a tempo
tenuto
8va
5
5
5
5
123
ff
sub. p
5
5
ff
sub. ppp
130
3
3
mp
3
p

139
tiring
take time
5
7
7
3
tiring
145
poco a poco dim.
poco a poco dim.
150
3
3
poco rit.
8va
3
3
poco rit.

158
Sultry, with a snap ♩ = 58
mp
pp
mp
ppp
p
ppp
mp
165
tr
with a snap
mf
mp
168
tr
p
mp a little eerie

172
tr
mf
p
175
secco
9
3
tr
178
ppp
10
8va
mf cantabile,
prominent
upper voice
15ma
pp from another world
take time
Ped.

181
(8)
11
10
(15)
183
8va
15ma
185
black keys
gliss.
mp
with loads of character
6

14

With newfound urgency ♩ = 90

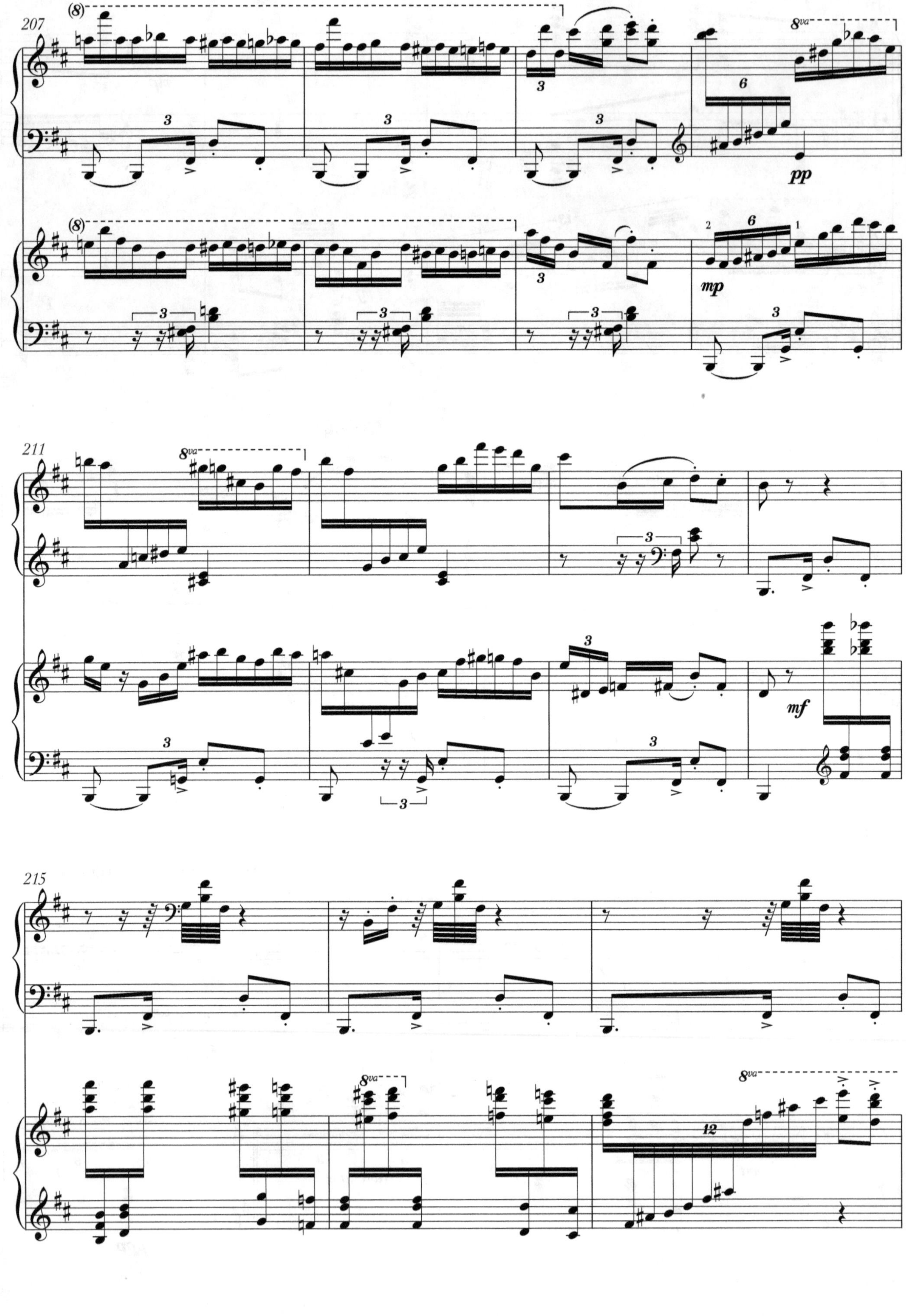
207
(8)
3
6
8va
pp
2
1
mp
211
mf
215
12

218
cresc.
mf
(8)
12
221
ff
10
reckless ff
sf
8vb
225
8va
f
5
fff with great gusto
8vb
tr
sf

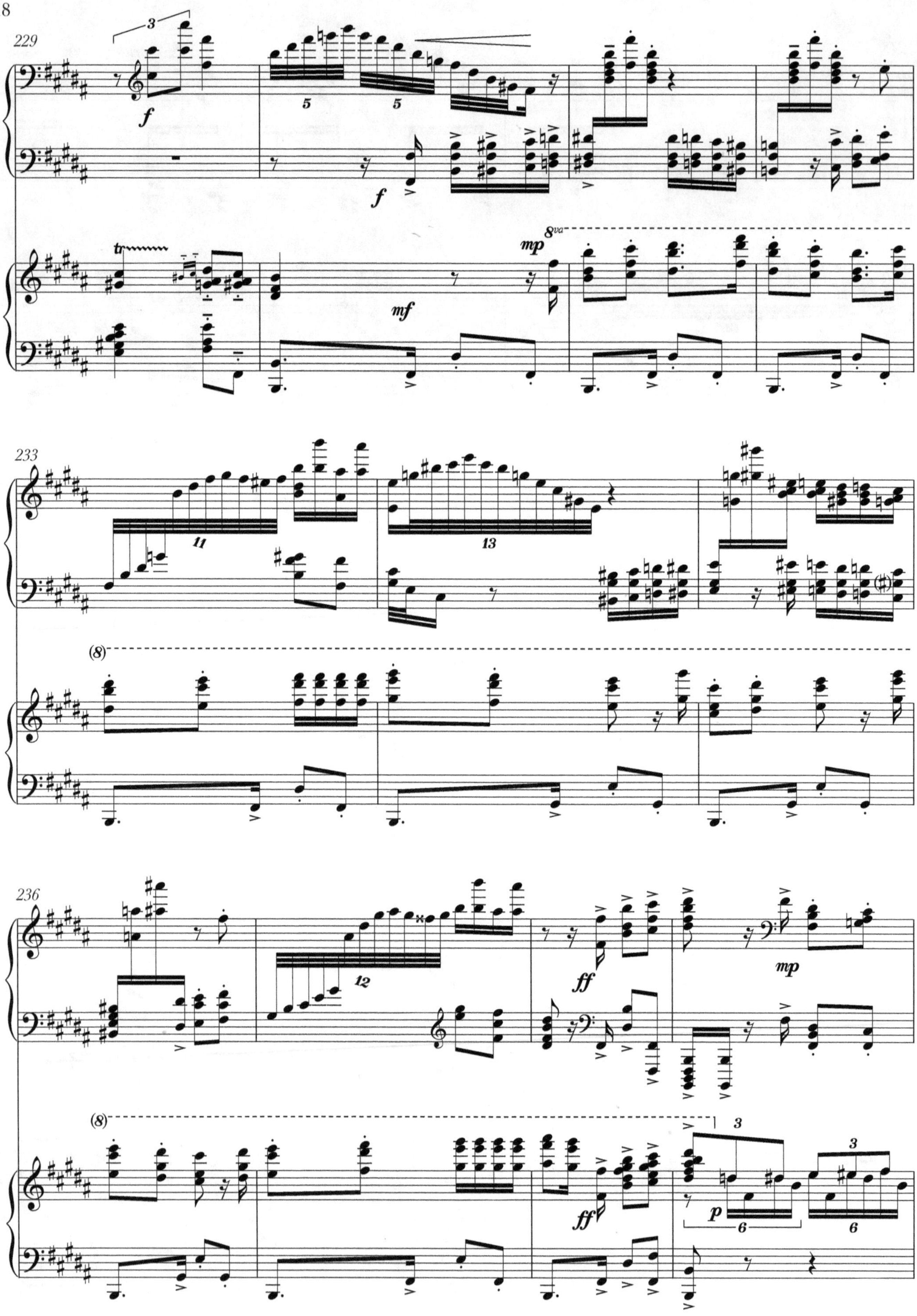
229
f
mf
mp
8va
233
11
13
(8)
236
12
ff
p

240
tr
ff
8vb
8va
3
6
9
f
244
8va
247
Andante molto
moderato ♩ = 58
p
8vb
8va

250

cantabile, espressivo, et sentimentale

mf

257

p shimmer

more

261

264
8va
266
articulate and with brewing energy
pp
mf
cantabile,
prominent L.H. melody
268
poco a poco cresc.
poco a poco cresc.

270

272

274

276
ff
impetuous
278
Soaring ♩ = 70
sub. p
molto
espressivo
rit.
cantabile, simple
283
cresc. and poco accel.
cresc. and poco accel.

286
mf cantabile
289
Poco più mosso ♩ = 80
mp
293
poco a poco dim.
poco a poco dim.

297
sempre dim.
cantabile
senza rit.
sempre dim.
senza rit.
Allegretto ♩ = 80, sempre accel.
302
p
articulate
p
articulate
307

312

317

Intense ♩ = 112, sempre accel.

p

sf *p* *but very intense*

322

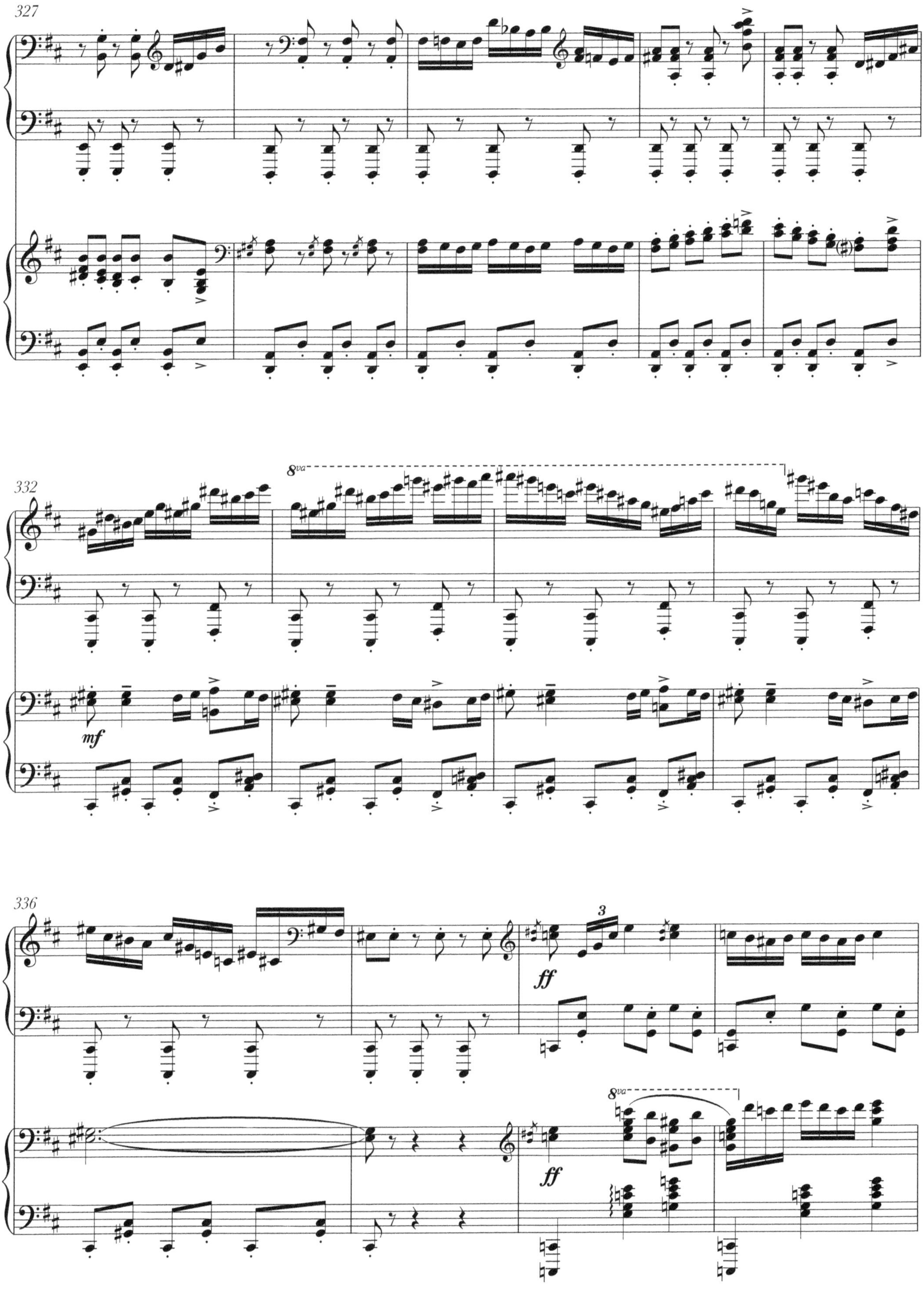
327
332
8va
mf
336
3
ff
8va
ff

340
pp
ff
3
8va
pp secco
ff
3
344
pp
p
♩ = 142, sempre accel.
8va
with flair
6
pp
p with flair
15ma
(8)
350
6
6
8va

354
mf
p
cresc.
358
sub. p
poco a poco cresc.
mf
sf
sf
363
f allargando
ff
ff allargando

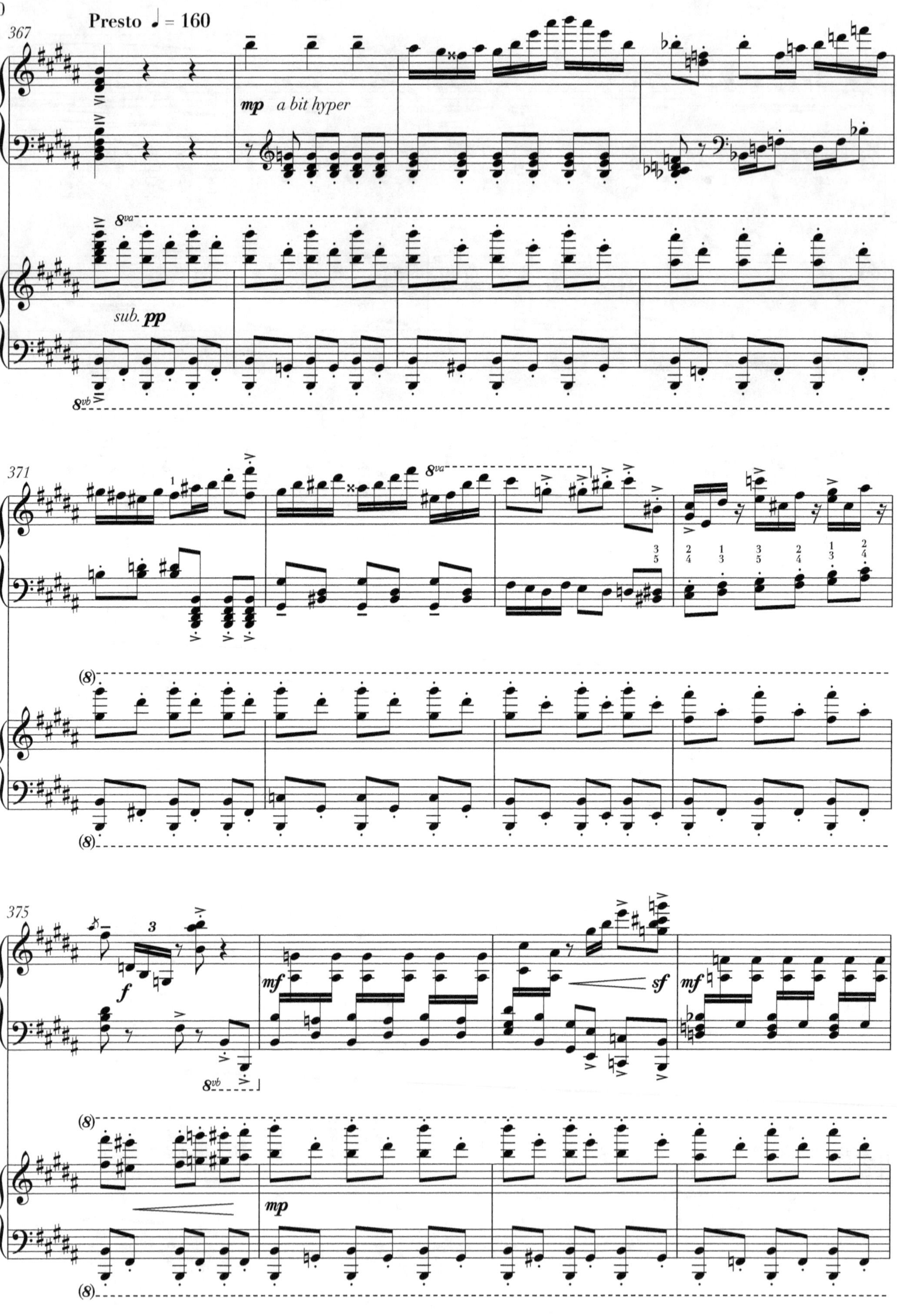
Presto ♩ = 160
367
mp a bit hyper
8va
sub. pp
8vb
371
375
f
mf
sf
mp

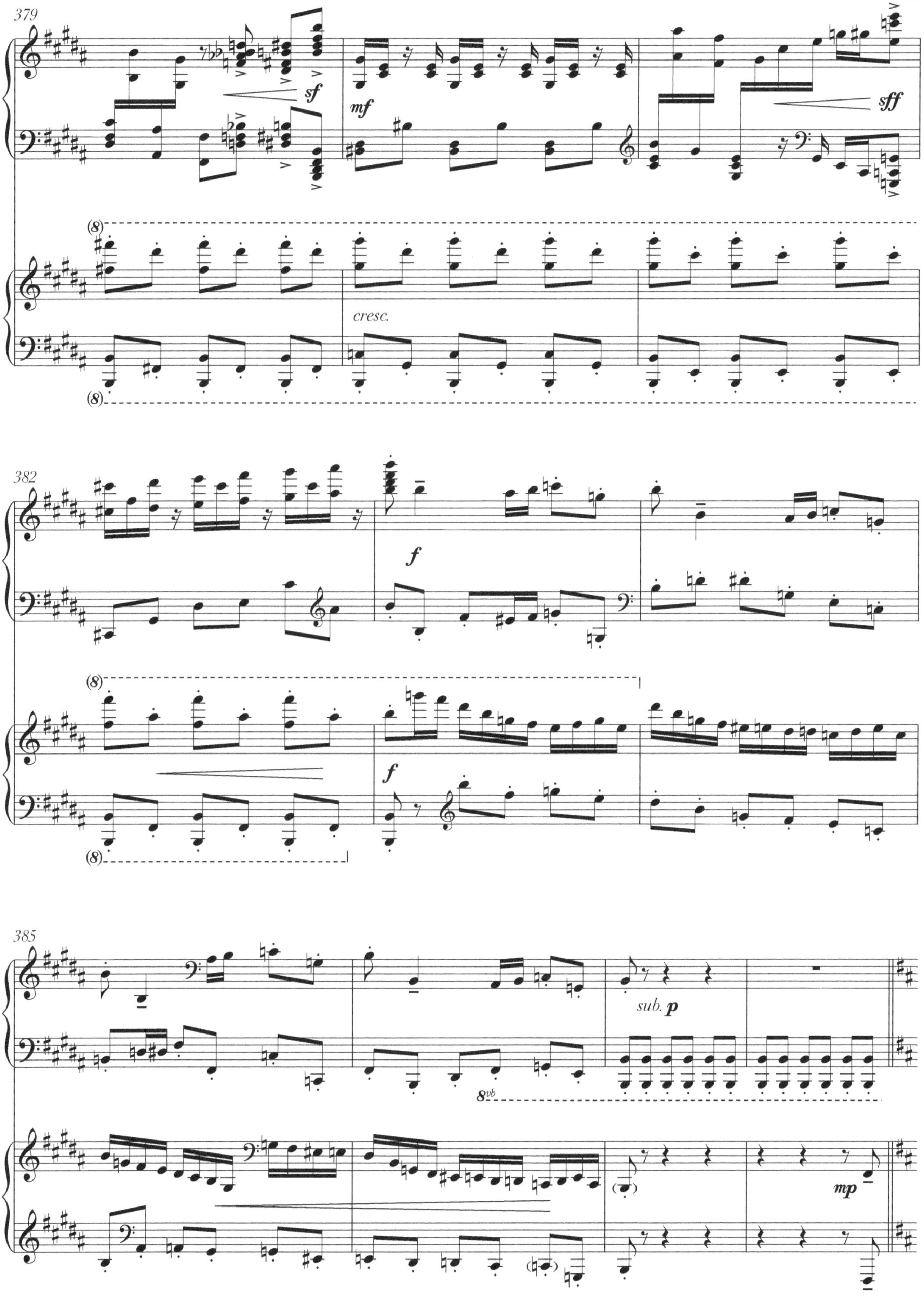
379
sf
mf
sff
(8)
cresc.
(8)
382
f
(8)
f
(8)
385
sub. p
8vb
mp

Piú Presto ♩ = 172
389
p
L.H. dry and crisp
(8)
pp
393
(8)
396
pp
mp
(8)
mf
p secco
L.H. dry and crisp
pp
8vb

400
p
403
p
406
poco allargando and cresc.
molto cresc.
8va
8vb
poco allargando and cresc.
molto cresc.

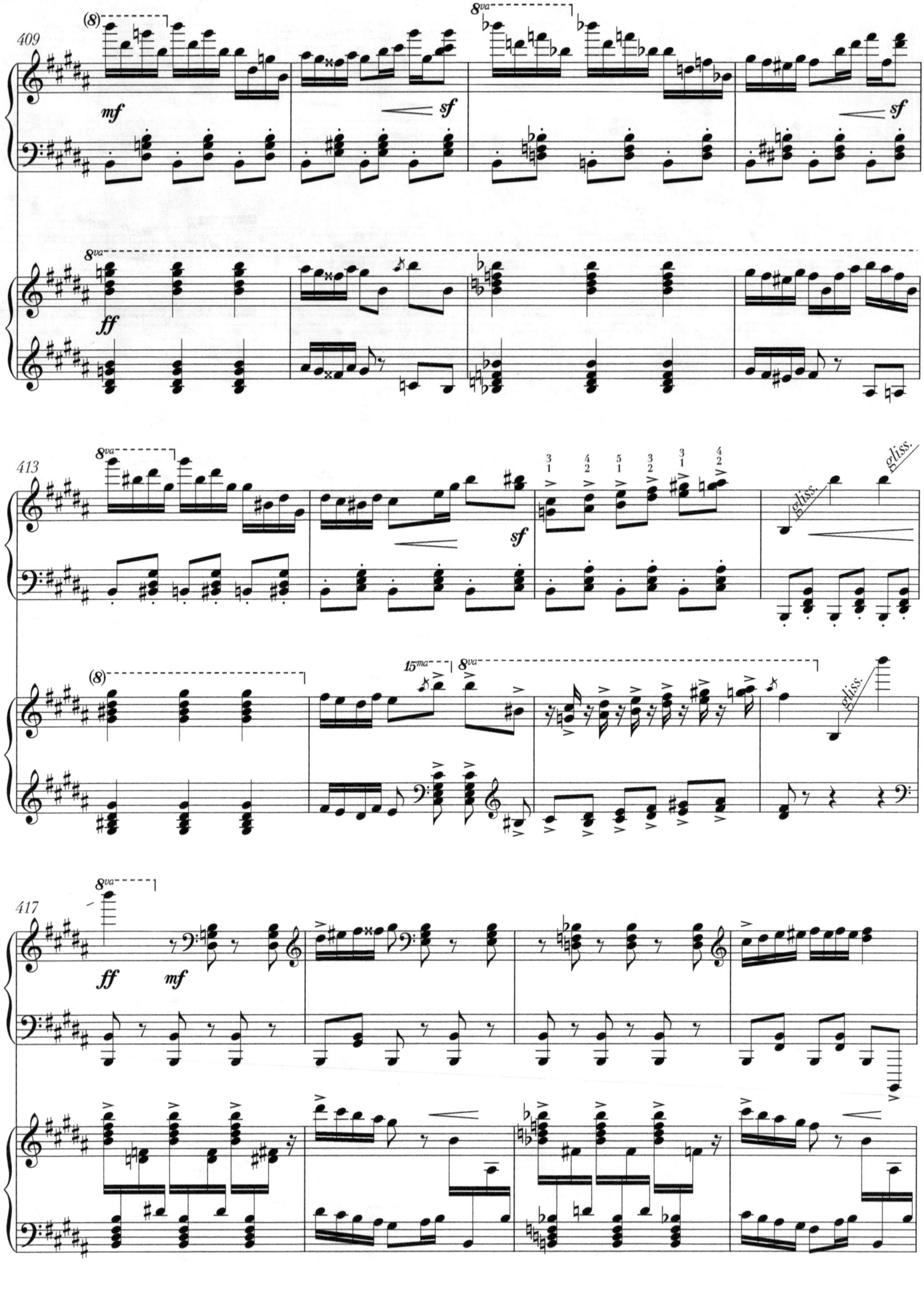
409
(8)
8va
mf
sf
ff
413
gliss.
15ma
417

421
sf
sub. mp
8va
sub. mp
425
accel. and cresc.
accel. and cresc.
gliss.
gliss.
Towering ♩ = 182
430
8va
fff
sf
sf
sf
8vb
sf
15ma
fff
8vb
sf

434
(8)
sf
sf
sf
sf
sf
438
(8)
sf
sf
sf
sub. mp
cresc.
sub. mp
cresc.
442
(8)
sf
1
sf

446
8va
broad
broad
450
8va
accel.
a tempo
8va
accel.
a tempo
8va
sf
8vb
454
tenuto
sf
8va
8va
8va
8va
tenuto
sf
sf
sf
sf
8vb

www.ingramcontent.com/pod-product-compliance
Lightning Source LLC
Chambersburg PA
CBHW05035710O426
42739CB00015BB/3434